ELECTRICITY

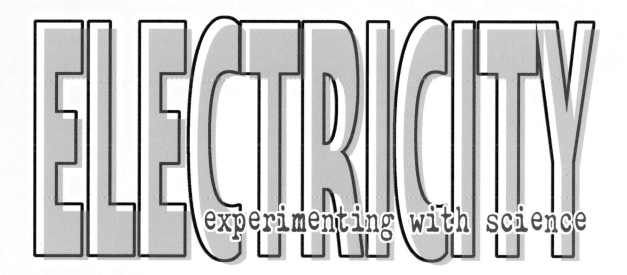

experimenting with science

Antonella Meiani

Lerner Publications Company • Minneapolis

First American edition published in 2003 by Lerner Publications Company

Published by arrangement with Istituto Geografico DeAgostini, Novara, Italy

Originally published as *Il Grande Libro degli Esperimenti*

Copyright © 1999 by Istituto Geografico DeAgostini, Novara, Italy

Translated from the Italian by Maureen Spurgeon.
Translation copyright © 2000 by Brown Watson, England.

This book has been adapted from a single-volume work entitled *Il Grande Libro degli Esperimenti*, originally published by Istituto Geografico DeAgostini, Novara, Italy, in 1999. New back matter was developed by Lerner Publications Company.

Lerner Publications Company
A division of Lerner Publishing Group
241 First Avenue North
Minneapolis, MN 55401 U.S.A.

Website address: www.lernerbooks.com

Library of Congress Cataloging-in-Publication Data

Meiani, Antonella.
　　[Il Grande libro degli esperimenti. English. Selections]
　　Electricity / by Antonella Meiani ; [translated from the Italian by Maureen Spurgeon]
　1st American ed.
　　　p.　cm. — (Experimenting with science)
　　Includes bibliographical references and index.
　　Summary: Experiments and text illustrate characteristics of static electricity, circuits and switches, and electrical currents.
　　ISBN: 0–8225–0086–8 (lib. bdg. : alk. paper)
　　1. Electricity—Experiments—Juvenile literature. [1. Electricity—Experiments.
　2. Experiments.] I. Title.
QC527.2.M4513　2003
537'.078—dc21
　　　　　　　　　　　　　　　　　　　　　　　　　　　　　　　2001050517

Manufactured in the United States of America
1 2 3 4 5 6 – JR – 08 07 06 05 04 03

Table of Contents

Electricity

What is lightning? Where does a current of electricity come from? How does a lamp light up?

You will find the answers to these questions and many more by doing the experiments in the next section, under the following headings:

- Static electricity
- Electric current
- Circuits and switches
- The effects of electrical current

Static electricity

The word *electricity* comes from the word *electron,* the name that the ancient Greeks gave to the mineral amber. They discovered that after amber was stroked on sheepskin it attracted lightweight objects, such as feathers and splinters of wood. At the end of the seventeenth century it was found that glass could also become "electrified," although in a different way. Since then, scientists have tried to discover all the secrets of electricity, tracing back to the structure of the atom. You too will be able to discover the effects of static electricity and understand what causes the little shocks that you feel on your hands, your clothes, and your hair. You will also learn how lightning strikes during a thunderstorm. All the experiments are safe to do, but an adult must be on hand to use some of the tools required.

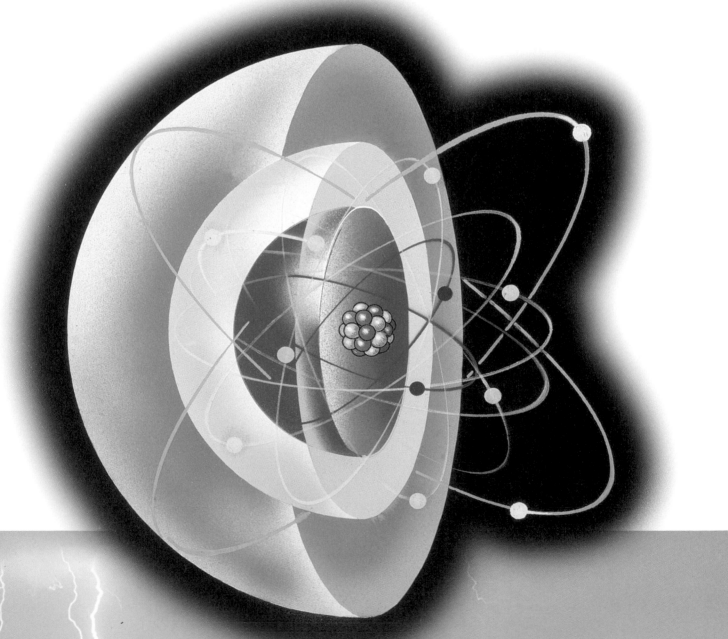

How can something be electrified?

SPECIAL POWERS

You need:
- balloon
- small pieces of thin paper
- wall
- faucet
- piece of woolen material

What to do:

1 Blow up the balloon. Stroke it vigorously with the woolen material.

2 Hold the balloon close to the pieces of paper, without touching them.

What happens?
The pieces of paper jump up and stick to the balloon.

3 Stroke the balloon again with the woolen cloth. Hold the balloon close to the wall.

What happens?
The balloon sticks to the wall.

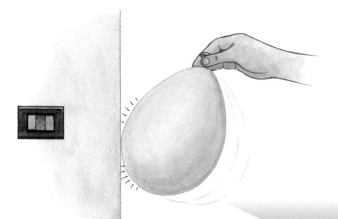

4 Turn on the faucet. Stroke the balloon again and move it near the stream of water.

What happens?
The jet of water curves and follows the movement of the balloon.

Why?
When you stroked the balloon with the woolen material it became electrified, with the power to attract things, almost like a magnet. Try holding the balloon near your hair and see how the hairs rise up, as if by magic.

The transfer of electrons
All matter is made up of tiny particles called *atoms*. Atoms contain even smaller particles, called *protons* and *electrons*, which each have an electrical charge. Protons have a *positive charge* (indicated by a + [plus] sign). Electrons have a *negative charge* (indicated by a – [minus] sign). Charges of the opposite sign attract. Charges of the same sign repel each other. Atoms contain an equal number of electrons and protons, so that each positive charge is balanced by a negative charge. Most atoms also have *neutrons*, particles without any electrical charge. Protons and neutrons make up the *nucleus* in the center of an atom. Electrons move continually around the nucleus. When we stroke a balloon with a woolen cloth, some electrons from the atoms in the wool enter the atoms of the balloon. Because the atoms of the balloon now have a greater number of electrons, the balloon becomes electrified.

A thing becomes electrified because the number of electrons in its atoms is either increased or decreased.

Why do some electrified objects attract and others repel?

BALLOON TEST

You need:
- two balloons
- length of thread
- woolen cloth
- piece of paper

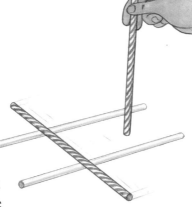

What to do:

1 Blow up the balloons. Tie the openings with the two ends of the thread.

2 Stroke both balloons with the woolen cloth.

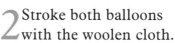

3 Hold the thread at the center and let the balloons hang down towards the floor.

What happens?
The two balloons move away from one another.

4 Now put the piece of paper between the two balloons.

What happens?
The two balloons move close together.

Why?
Objects made of the same material acquire the same electrical charge, and electrical charges of the same type repel. The balloons, which both have a negative charge, move apart. The paper, which is not electrified, has the same number of negative and positive charges. It is the positive charges that attract the negative charges of the balloon.

MOVING STRAWS

You need:
- four plastic drinking straws
- glass rod
- woolen cloth
- table

What to do:

1 Put two straws parallel on the table, 5 cm (2 in.) apart.

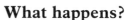

2 Stroke the other two straws with the woolen cloth. Place one across the first two straws. Bring the fourth straw near to the others, first from the left, then from the right. Be careful not to touch the other straws.

What happens?
The drinking straw placed on the first two straws rolls forward and then back, as if it is being pushed by the electrified straw.

3 Stroke the glass rod with the woolen cloth. Repeat the experiment.

What happens?
The straw rolls towards the glass rod, and follows it as you move the rod away.

Why?
The straw has a negative charge, while stroking the glass rod with the cloth gives it a positive charge. The two plastic straws, having the same charge, repel. The glass and the plastic, having opposite charges, attract each other.

A MAGIC STICK

You need:
- drinking straw
- square piece of thin paper
- toothpick
- woolen cloth
- eraser
- scissors

What to do:

1 Fold the piece of paper into quarters, and cut as shown in the picture. When you unfold the paper, you will have a star shape.

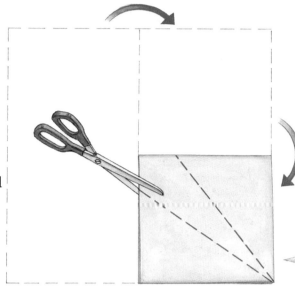

2 Stick the toothpick into the eraser. Place the center of the paper star on the point of the toothpick.

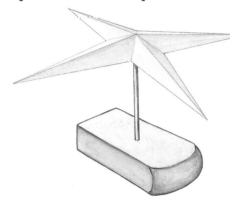

What happens?
The star turns to follow the movement of the drinking straw.

3 Stroke the drinking straw with the woolen cloth. Then move the straw around the top of the star, as if drawing circles around it.

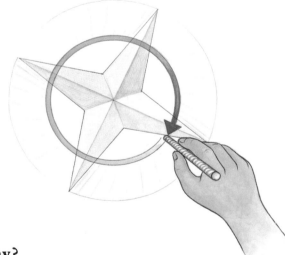

Why?
Stroking with the woolen cloth has given the straw a negative electrical charge. So the straw can attract the opposite (positive) charges of the paper. That is why the star follows the movement of the straw.

Electrical charges can be positive or negative. Charges of the same type repel. Opposite charges attract.

How is an object's electrical charge determined?

You need:
- objects of different materials (plastic, metal, wood, paper) to test
- plastic pen
- glass rod
- thread
- cotton cloth
- silk cloth
- woolen cloth

What to do:

1 Using the thread, hang the plastic pen and the glass rod from sticks. Keep them a good distance from each other.

2 Stroke the pen and the rod with one of the cloths.

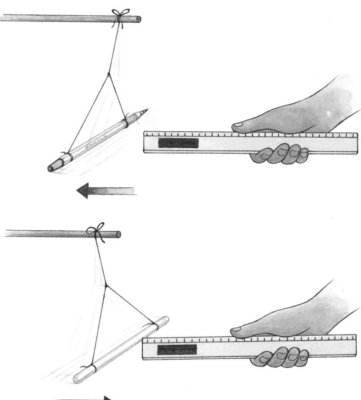

3 Stroke each test object with the cloth and bring each one near the pen in turn. Then hold each object near the glass rod.

What happens?
Each object is electrified by stroking with the cloth. This causes the object to be repelled by one of the charged objects (the pen or the rod) and to attract the other.

Why?
The plastic pen has a negative charge. The glass rod has a positive charge. From this, we know that the objects that attract the plastic pen and repel the glass rod have a positive charge. Those that cause the opposite effect have a negative charge.

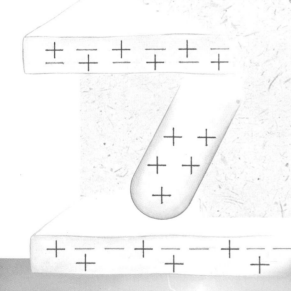

Induction and contact

An object with a neutral electrical charge has no overall charge. Its charges are distributed evenly (top diagram). The charges separate when the object is touched by an electrified object, because the electrified object attracts opposite charges (bottom diagram). The neutral object is temporarily electrified by induction. When the two objects are separated, the charges of the neutral object once again distribute themselves evenly.

If we touch the neutral object with an electrified object with a positive charge, it will attract the neutral object's negative charges. But such electrification by contact does not last.

BUILD AN ELECTROSCOPE

You need:
- glass jar
- cork that fits tightly enough to seal the jar
- a length of iron wire
- strip of aluminum foil
- glass rod and plastic rod
- woolen cloth

Once the experiment has been set up, be careful not to touch the iron wire with your hand, or the electrical charge will be lost.

What to do:

1 Thread the wire through the center of the cork so that it sticks out at the top and at the bottom. Bend the bottom end, as shown in the picture.

2 Fold the strip of foil in half. Hang the foil on the bottom end of the wire. Place the cork in the top of the jar.

3 Stroke the plastic rod with the woolen cloth. Then touch the top end of the wire with the plastic rod.

What happens?
The two "fins" of the foil spread apart.

4 Now electrify the glass rod by stroking it with the woolen cloth. Touch the top wire with the glass rod.

What happens?
The foil "fins" close together.

Why?
The contact between the plastic rod and the wire causes the negative charge of the plastic to be transmitted through the wire to the two halves of the foil. As they acquire the negative charge, they repel. When you touch the wire with the glass rod, the positive charge of the glass rod neutralizes the negative charge of the foil and the two halves close again. The same thing happens when you touch the wire first with the glass rod and then with the plastic rod.

The instrument you have made is an *electroscope*, used to detect a positive or negative charge. You can repeat the experiment, charging your electroscope each time with a negative charge (by contact with the plastic) or a positive charge (by contact with the glass). Then test objects of different materials that have been electrified by stroking.

Why does the charge go away?
By doing these experiments, you will find that electrification of an object goes away after a time. This happens because electrons are attracted by atoms in the air, or in anything that touches the electrified object (such as a hand or a shelf), and this changes the balance between the charges.

Charges that are like those in the charged glass are positive.
Charges that are like those in the charged plastic are negative.

What is lightning?

ARTIFICIAL LIGHTNING

You need:
- large, flat baking dish
- large handful of modeling clay
- sheet of plastic
- coin
- dark room

What to do:

1 Soften the clay and stick it down in the center of the dish. The clay must be stuck down firmly enough for you to be able to lift the baking dish with it.

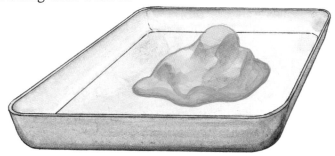

2 Place the baking dish on the sheet of plastic. Then, holding the clay, rub the dish vigorously on the plastic for about one minute.

3 Still holding the clay, lift up the baking dish and take it into the dark room. Be careful not to touch the baking dish with your hands.

4 In the dark room, hold a coin close to the corner of the dish.

What happens?
The contact between the coin and the dish produces a spark.

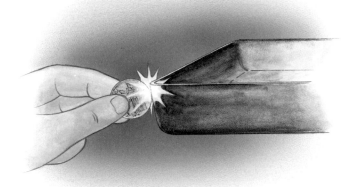

Why?
Having been stroked on the plastic, the baking dish is electrified with a negative charge. When you brought the coin close to it, the excess charges were quickly transferred through the air, from the sheet to the coin and to your body. (You will have felt a slight shock.) The passage through the air was visible as the spark. This experiment reproduces in miniature a flash of lightning in a storm.

Electricity in the sky

During a storm, the lower parts of the clouds, having been rubbed by masses of air, become charged with negative electricity. This accumulation of negative electricity in the clouds attracts positive charges on Earth's surface (on trees, houses, and large structures, for example). When the negative charge of the clouds is strong enough, lightning strikes – a short transfer of electrical charge from the clouds to the ground or between one cloud and another. Lightning is seen as a flash of light and heard as thunder – because of a buildup of heat, the air expands suddenly, causing a loud rumble.

The invention of the lightning rod

The lightning rod was invented by Benjamin Franklin in 1752. He believed that lightning was an enormous electrical charge and was convinced that a metal point would attract this charge. To prove his theory, Franklin built a kite with an iron tip, and threaded a key on the end of the string of the kite. He tried out his kite during a violent storm. The kite and its wet string became electrically charged. In fact, when Franklin touched the key, it gave him an electric shock! Following this experiment, Franklin built the first lightning rod, a metal pole with a very high point that he put in his garden. During storms, lots of sparks were seen around its tip. This metal pole attracted most of the electrical charge from the clouds before it reached the ground, avoiding damage to houses and other structures.

Modern lightning rods have a metal wire leading to the ground, which enables electrical charges to descend and disperse safely in the soil.

Lightning is an electrical charge traveling from a highly electrified cloud to Earth.

Electric current

Another quality of electricity is its ability to move, to run along pre-set courses called circuits. But how can electricity move from one object to another? And from what materials is a circuit made? Can electricity flow through anything? Why do we call the force that we use to switch on a light a current? By using simple batteries in the next set of experiments, you will be able to work safely to understand how it is possible to tame such a powerful and dangerous force as electricity so that we can use it every day.

How is an electric current generated?

A PATH CALLED A CIRCUIT

You need:
- 4.5-volt battery
- two pieces of insulated (plastic-covered) electric cable
- small lightbulb
- wire cutters

What to do:

1 Use the wire cutters to peel off the plastic from both ends of the cables. (Ask an adult to do this for you). Be careful not to cut into the small wires inside.

2 Wind one uncovered end of each piece of cable around a battery contact, as shown.

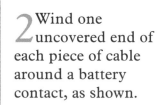

3 Place the two free ends of wire on the bulb. One wire must touch the bottom of the metal base and the other must touch the side of the base.

What happens?
The bulb lights up.

Why?
What you saw transformed into the light energy of the bulb was the electrical current. This is a flow of electrical charge conducted from the battery through the wires and into the bulb, along a set course called a circuit.

When does electricity move?

Electrical current is generated when extra electrons in an electrified object are free to move towards an object that is less charged. This difference in charge between one object and another is called potential difference, or voltage. The battery maintains a certain difference in potential between one end of the circuit and the other.

A CONTINUOUS COURSE

You need:
- 4.5-volt battery
- three pieces of insulated electric cable
- small lightbulb
- wire cutters
- bulb holder

What to do:

1 Ask an adult to peel away the plastic from the ends of the pieces of wire, using the wire cutters. (Be careful not to cut the copper wires inside!)

2 Put the bulb in the bulb holder, so that you do not have to hold the bulb in your hand.

3 Connect the battery, the two wires, and the bulb holder, as in the picture.

4 Alternately bring into contact and then move apart the two free ends of the electric cable.

What happens?
When the wires touch, the bulb lights up. When they are apart, it remains unlit.

Why?
The circuit (the route along which the electricity flows from the battery) must be closed (unbroken) for it to work. If a circuit is open (broken), the current of electricity cannot flow through it.

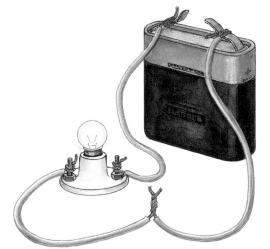

When electrical charges move in a circuit between two objects, the objects have a certain difference in potential.

Can electricity flow through all substances?

CONDUCTORS OF ELECTRICITY

You need:
- 4.5-volt battery
- 5-volt lightbulb in a bulb holder
- three pieces of insulated electric cable (with the ends uncovered, as in the last two experiments)
- two metal brackets
- two screws that fit the holes in the brackets
- small piece of wood
- some objects to test: a nail, a strip of rubber, a toothpick, a strip of aluminum foil, a glass rod, a leather shoelace, a drinking straw

What to do:

1 Screw the two brackets onto the wood, about 2 cm (1 in.) apart.

2 Place the bulb holder next to the brackets and connect the battery, the bulb holder, and the two brackets with the three pieces of electric cable, as shown in the picture.

3 Place each test object, one at a time, across the brackets.

What happens?
The nail and the aluminum foil make the bulb light up. The other objects do not.

Why?
The bulb lights up only when an object made of metal is placed across the metal brackets. The metal object closes the circuit and allows the current to flow. Rubber, plastic, wood, glass, and leather are insulators, which means that these materials do not let the electrical charge pass through them. Insulating materials are used as protection from electricity. Electric cable, for example, is covered with plastic so that it can be touched on the outside without the handler getting an electric shock.

Insulators and conductors

In substances that conduct electricity, there are electrons that are free to move because they are not strongly attracted to their atoms. Such electrons are able to transport electricity from one place to another. On the other hand, the electrons in insulators are strongly attracted to their atoms. The electrons do not conduct electricity because they cannot move around. The ability of an object to conduct electricity is indicated by the term resistance. The less resistance an object has against the flow of the electricity, the greater its ability to conduct a current.

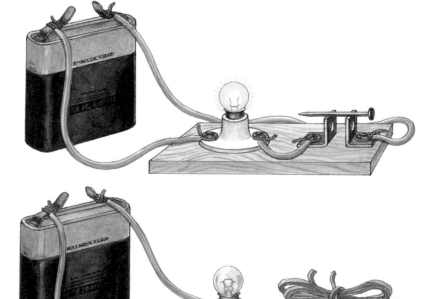

WINNING CONNECTIONS

You need:
- piece of strong cardboard
- sheet of paper
- ten brass fasteners
- electric cable
- wire cutters
- 4.5-volt battery
- small lightbulb with bulb holder
- glue
- pencil
- scissors

What to do:

1 Cut ten rectangles from the paper. On these write the names of five states and their five capital cities. Then paste them in two columns on the cardboard, so that the states are not next to their capital cities.

2 Make a hole in the cardboard next to each name. Thread a brass fastener through each hole.

3 Ask an adult to cut five pieces of electric cable and strip the ends with wire cutters. On the back of the cardboard, use the wires to connect each state with its correct capital city. (Wind the wire around the metal fins of each brass fastener.)

4 With another piece of electric cable, connect a battery contact with one side of the bulb holder. Take another two pieces of wire. Connect one to the other battery contact and the second to the free side of the bulb holder. The other two ends of these wires will be left free.

5 Invite a friend to try matching up the right state with the right capital city, using the free ends of the wires.

What happens?
If the connection is correct, the bulb will light up. If the connection is wrong, the bulb remains unlit.

Why?
The fasteners are made of brass, a metal and a conductor of electricity. If the player's wires touch two brass fasteners that are connected at the back, the circuit closes and the electricity that flows through lights up the bulb. If the wires are placed next to a state and a capital city that do not match, the circuit remains open and the bulb does not light up.

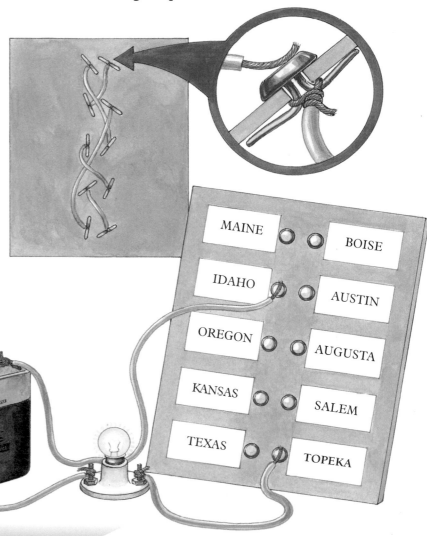

Some materials are conductors of electricity. They allow current to pass through them. Others are insulators. They stop the flow.

Can water conduct electricity?

DIFFERENT REACTIONS

You need:
- glass or plastic container
- two small terminals (clamps)
- electric cable
- 4.5-volt battery
- lightbulb
- distilled water (from a garage or grocery store)
- salt
- wire cutters

What to do:

1 Fill the container with distilled water.

2 Ask an adult to cut three pieces of cable. Strip the ends. Connect two wires to the battery contacts, and connect one of the free ends to a terminal. Connect one end of the third wire to the other terminal.

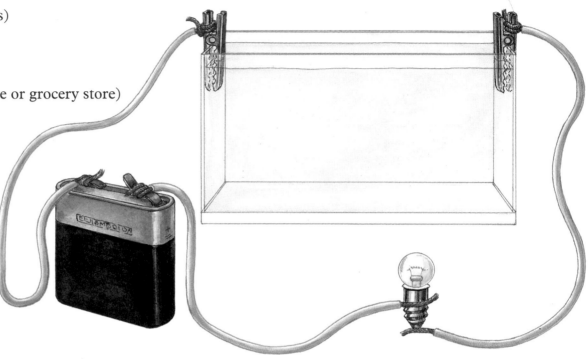

3 Place a terminal on each side of the container, so that they touch the water.

4 Touch the free ends of the wires to the lightbulb, one touching the bottom of the metal base, and the other touching the side of the base.

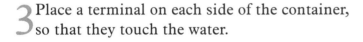

Dangers of electricity

You must NEVER touch switches or electrical equipment that is switched on if you have wet hands, or if you are standing with bare feet on a wet surface. The water in our homes is not distilled and is therefore a good conductor of electricity. So if an electric current flows through the water, it can give you a very serious electric shock.

What happens?
The lightbulb does not light up.

5 Add a few handfuls of salt to the water. Touch the wires to the lightbulb as before.

What happens?
The lightbulb lights up.

Why?
The distilled water is an insulator, which means that it prevents the flow of the electrical charge. But if you add salt to the water, it becomes a conductor. When the salt dissolves, the particles in it, being electrically charged, are attracted to the terminals connected to the battery. This creates a sort of connection that closes the circuit and allows the electricity to pass through.

Pure water is an insulator, but water containing salt is a good conductor of electricity.

Why is the position of the battery important?

PAY ATTENTION TO THE SIGNS

You need:
- two 1.5-volt batteries
- small lightbulb
- two pieces of electric cable with the ends uncovered
- ruler
- tape

What to do:

1 Tape the two batteries along the length of the ruler as shown in the picture. Put a positive pole (the end marked with a plus [+] sign) next to a negative pole (the end marked with a minus [−] sign).

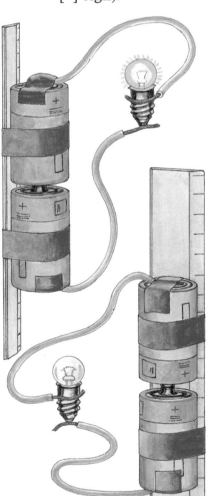

2 Tape the ends of the two wires to the opposite ends of the batteries. Then touch the lightbulb with the free ends of the wires, as shown.

What happens?
The bulb lights up.

3 Now reverse the position of the batteries, so that the two positive poles touch.

4 Re-connect the wires to the two ends of the batteries. Touch the lightbulb again.

What happens?
The bulb does not light up.

Why?
Electrons flow continually from the negative pole to the positive pole of a battery. The same thing happens if two batteries are connected to each other, because the electrons still escape from the negative pole of one battery and go towards the positive pole of the other.

If two negative poles or positive poles are next to one another, the current cannot flow from negative to positive. This is why a flashlight or toy will not work if a battery is inserted with the poles in the wrong positions.

The invention of Alessandro Volta

The first electrical battery was invented by the Italian scientist Alessandro Volta towards the end of the eighteenth century. It consisted of a series of zinc and copper discs, separated from each other by discs of material soaked in a solution of water and sulfuric acid. The discs were piled vertically, one on top of the other. By connecting the first disc of zinc and the last disc of copper with copper wire, Volta obtained a continuous passage of electrical current, due to the chemical reaction between the zinc and the acid solution. The current was broken only when the acid was used up.

Volta also discovered that a flow of current was created each time two different conductors were installed, with a suitable contact between them.

The current generated by batteries can flow only between poles of opposite signs.

Circuits and switches

Switching the television on and off, and the computer, the hair dryer, all the lights at home . . . how many switches do we use each day? What is behind all those toggles and buttons that we click? A switch is an extremely simple device, but one that is impossible to do without! A switch is a small bridge that closes a circuit that has been temporarily broken. It allows us to use electrical equipment whenever we need it. Follow the experiments in this section, and you can try making your own switches.

Can a circuit light up more than one lightbulb?

DIFFERENT CIRCUITS

You need:
- two 4.5-volt batteries
- four lightbulbs, each with a bulb holder
- electric cable
- wire cutters (Remember that each time you cut a piece of wire, you must strip the plastic off both ends; ask an adult to do this.)

What to do:

1 Connect one bulb to one of the batteries. Note the brightness of the light that it gives off.

2 Connect two lightbulbs to the same battery, as shown in the picture.

What happens?
The two lightbulbs give out light that is not as bright as one bulb alone.

Why?
The two lightbulbs share the same energy, which passed from one to the other. What you have built is called a series circuit. If you disconnect one of the two bulbs, the circuit will be broken and the other bulb will go out.

3 Connect a bulb holder to the contacts of the second battery. Then connect another bulb holder to the first, as shown in the picture.

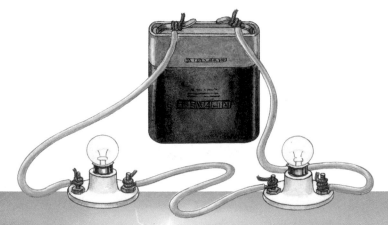

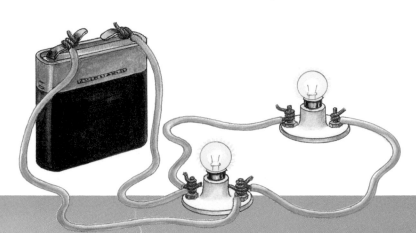

What happens?

The two lightbulbs each give off the same amount of light as when only one bulb was connected to the battery.

Why?

Each lightbulb is on its own circuit that is fed directly from the battery. This type of circuit is called a parallel circuit. If one of the bulbs burns out or is disconnected, the other continues to shine because its own circuit is not broken.

A short circuit

If it is not kept under control, an electrical current can cause damage and lead to danger. One of the most common faults is the short circuit. If you were to take a short length of the insulating plastic coating off each of the wires connecting the battery to the lightbulb and put the bare wires in contact with each other, you would see them giving off sparks, and the lightbulb would go out. In a short circuit, the current returns directly to the battery without passing through the lightbulb, completing a circuit that is shorter. Not meeting any resistance on this circuit, the current becomes more intense (stronger) and so produces a lot of heat. In electrical installations, a short circuit can cause fires or seriously damage the installation. To avoid this, we use "safety valves" called fuses and circuit breakers. When there is an overload of current in the circuit, or the current is too strong, the wire in a fuse will break, or the circuit breaker will switch off, breaking the circuit.

One circuit can power more than one lightbulb continuously, whether connected in series or in parallel.

Why do we need switches?

A DEVICE FOR LIGHT

You need:
- small piece of wood
- two metal thumbtacks
- metal paper clip
- three pieces of insulated electric cable with the plastic stripped off the ends (Ask an adult to do this.)
- lightbulb with a bulb holder
- 4.5-volt battery

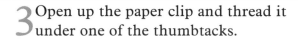

What to do:

1 Stick the two thumbtacks in the piece of wood, about 3–4 cm (1–2 in.) apart from each other.

2 Attach a wire to each thumbtack. Connect the free end of one of the wires to a battery contact and the free end of the other wire to the bulb holder. Connect the third wire from the bulb holder to the other battery contact, as shown.

3 Open up the paper clip and thread it under one of the thumbtacks.

4 Move the other end of the paper clip and bring it into contact with the second thumbtack. Then push the end of the paper clip away from the second thumbtack.

What happens?
When the paper clip touches both thumbtacks, the bulb lights up. When the paper clip is moved away, the contact is broken and the bulb remains unlit.

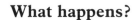

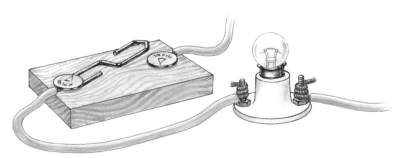

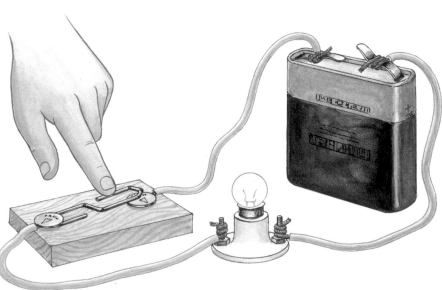

Why?
The paper clip is made of metal, which is a conductor of electricity. So when it touches both thumbtacks, the circuit closes and allows the passage of the electrical current. When the paper clip is moved away from the second thumbtack, the circuit is open and the current is interrupted.

MESSAGE IN CODE

You need:
- two small pieces of wood
- two lightbulbs, each with a bulb holder
- eight pieces of electric cable, with the plastic stripped off the ends (Ask an adult to do this.)
- four metal thumbtacks
- two metal paper clips
- two 4.5-volt batteries
- paper
- pen

What to do:

1 Make two electrical circuits exactly the same as for the last experiment. Connect the two bulbs with wires that are long enough for the two bulbs to be in different rooms.

2 With a friend, work out a code along the same lines as Morse code, with each letter of the alphabet corresponding to a series of long or short flashes of light.

3 Send your friend a short message from one room to the other. When he or she has the switch open, then you can signal with yours. For each short flash, press the paper clip against the thumbtack quickly. For each long flash, hold the paper clip against the thumbtack a little longer.

What happens?
Your friend will receive your message in the form of light signals. If you leave your switch open, he or she can then send an answer in the same way.

Why?
Each time the paper clip touches the thumbtack, the circuit closes and the bulb lights up. The longer the contact, the longer the light stays on.

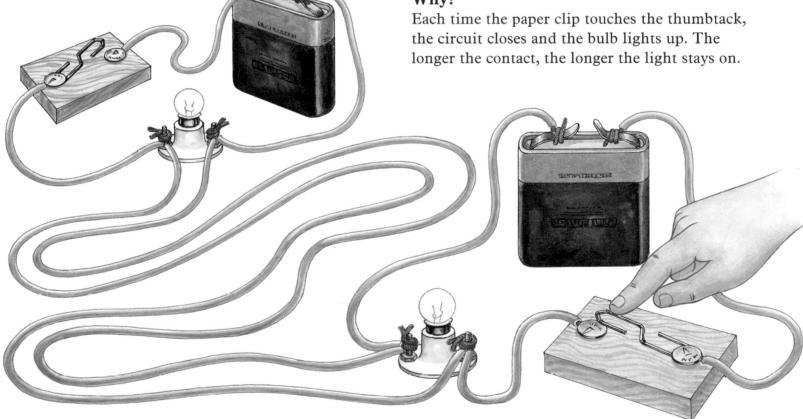

A switch either closes or opens an electrical circuit.

What is a current gate?

A TWO-WAY SWITCH

You need:
- electric cable
- six metal thumbtacks
- two paper clips
- 4.5-volt battery
- two small pieces of wood
- lightbulb and bulb holder

What to do:

1 Push three thumbtacks into each piece of wood, as you see in the picture.

2 On each piece of wood, open up a paper clip and place one end under the center thumbtack. In this way, the paper clip can be moved to touch either of the other two thumbtacks.

3 Using the electric cable, connect the switches to the battery and the lightbulb, as shown in the bottom picture.

4 Try out different positions of the switches to light up or to turn off the lightbulb.

What happens?
The lightbulb can be lit or turned off by either of the two switches.

Why?
When both switches and the wire form an unbroken circuit, the current passes through the circuit and the bulb lights up. If either one of the two paper clips is moved, this opens the circuit and makes the light go out.

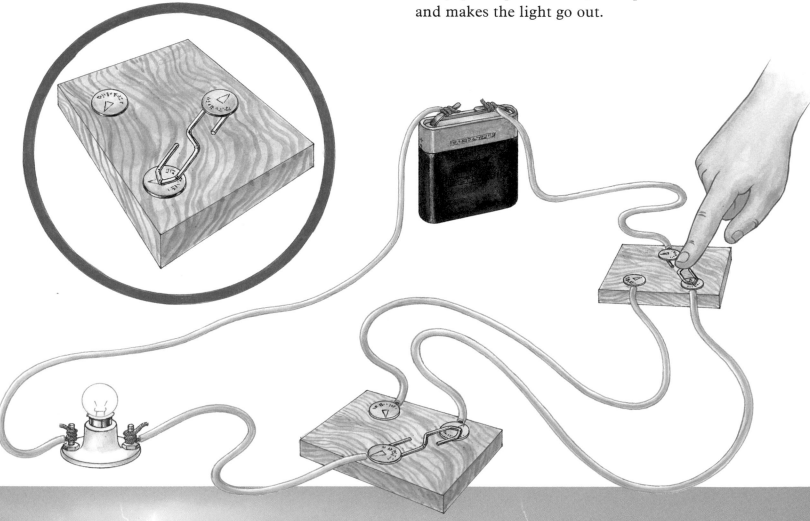

Electric switches in the home

When a room has two doors, it may be necessary to be able to switch the same light on and off from different points near each door. In this case, an electrical installation must be equipped with a two-way switch, like the one that you made in the last experiment. The same system can be used to switch the light on and off both at the bottom and the top of a staircase.

Switches and microcircuits

Inside a computer there are complicated electrical circuits called integrated circuits (shown in the photograph), built on a coating of silicon (a material that is very light and resistant) just a few millimeters thick. The tiny switches of these circuits are called transistors. They allow the current to pass from one circuit to another. Transistors are like little doors that open and close according to the impulses that we transmit through the computer. Each time we tap in a command on the keyboard, the computer translates it into electrical impulses. When an impulse arrives at a transistor, the transistor activates or deactivates the circuit to which it is connected, depending on the strength of the impulse. Through this circulation of electrical impulses the computer processes the data we input and responds according to its programming. Transistors are not only the smallest switches ever invented, they are also the fastest. They can open and close thousands of times in one minute!

A current gate allows an electrical circuit to open or close in one of two different directions.

The effects of electrical current

Can you imagine what everyday life would be like without electricity? Try to think how many jobs are made possible only because of electrical current! We use electricity for lighting; for heating, refrigeration and air conditioning; to power motors; for travel in trains; in our play... so many things around us use the many effects of electricity.

You already know that an electric lightbulb heats up soon after it is turned on. But did you also know that a small electric shock can transform some substances into others? The next section of experiments will show you how this happens.

How does a bulb light up?

GLOWING WIRE

You need:
- thin piece of wood
- two thin nails
- steel filament (You can unravel this from a steel scouring pad.)
- two pieces of electric cable with the plastic stripped off the ends
- 4.5-volt battery

What to do:

1 Tap the two nails into the wood. Wind an end of the steel filament around the base of each nail.

2 Wind one end of a cable around a battery contact, and the other end around a nail, above the filament. Connect a second cable to the other battery contact. Touch the free end to the other nail. Keep your hand away from the filament!

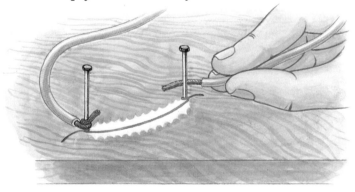

What happens?
The steel filament becomes red.

Why?
The electrical current flows easily through the electric cable. But it is more difficult for it to flow through the steel filament. That is why the flow of electricity heats up the filament and makes it change color.

BRIGHTNESS THAT VANISHES

You need:
- 4.5-volt battery
- lightbulb with bulb holder
- electric cable with uncovered ends
- new pencil with both ends sharpened to a point
- tape

What to do:

1 Connect the lightbulb to the battery with the electric cable, as before. Observe the light.

2 Insert the pencil into the circuit, taping the wires to the lead of the points.

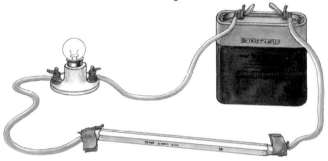

What happens?
The light from the bulb is not as bright.

Why?
The graphite in the lead conducts the current, but offers some resistance to the flow. As it resists the flow, the graphite absorbs part of the electricity and so the lightbulb dims.

How a lightbulb is made

Inside an electric lightbulb is a thin metal spiral, supported by two filaments that are also made of metal. The electricity enters the bulb and flows through the wire. But the spiral wire does not let the electricity pass through easily, because of its size and because of the material of which it is made. The force of the current causes the filament to heat up, and the hot filament gives off a white light.

The filament inside a lightbulb offers some resistance to the flow of the current. So the filament heats up and gives off light.

Does electricity always produce heat?

THE HEAT OF ELECTRICITY

You need:
- thermometer
- 4.5-volt battery
- length of thin copper wire
- insulating tape

What to do:
1 Wind the copper wire around the bulb of the thermometer, so that the spirals do not touch. The loose ends of the wire should be fairly long. If necessary, you can secure the wire on the thermometer with the insulating tape.

2 Wind the ends of the wire around the battery contacts.

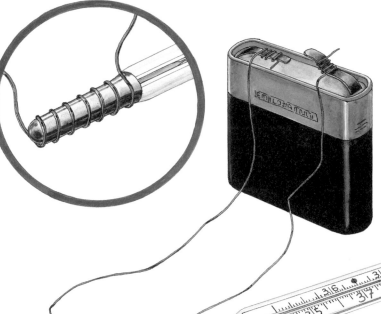

What happens?
After a few minutes, the temperature rises on the thermometer.

Why?
The electrical current that flows through the wire produces heat.

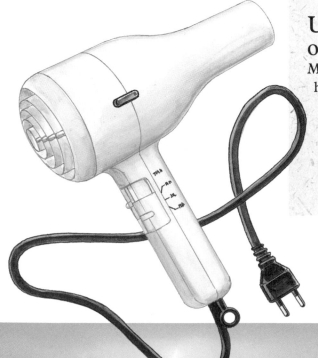

Using the heating effects of electricity
Many electrical items that we use in our homes have electrical resistance that heats them up with the passage of the current and changes the electrical energy into thermal (heat) energy. This is what happens with things like electric irons, electric skillets, toasters, electric blankets, and hair dryers.

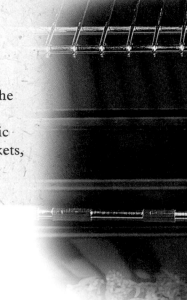

TRANSFORMATION OF ENERGY

You need:

- three 4.5-volt batteries
- electric cable with the ends uncovered, as before
- small piece of wood with two metal thumbtacks stuck into it
- strip of aluminum foil

What to do:

1 Connect the three batteries and the piece of wood with the thumbtacks as illustrated in the picture. (Be sure that the poles that are connected have opposite signs.)

2 Place the strip of foil across the two thumbtacks.

3 Now cut the foil to make it narrower. Put the foil across the thumbtacks once again.

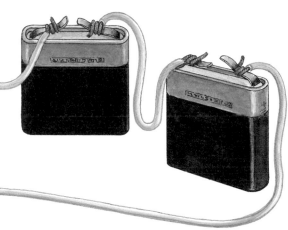

What happens?

The aluminum heats up. It becomes even hotter when it is narrower.

Why?

The strip of foil offers resistance to the passage of current and transforms part of the electrical energy into heat. The thinner the strip, the more difficult the passage of the electrical current, and the more heat that is generated. Even in normal electric bulbs, brightness comes from the energy that flows through the filament into the bulb and becomes transformed into heat. That is why a lightbulb is too hot to touch only moments after the power has been switched on.

Part of the electrical energy that goes through a conductor is always transformed into heat.

What does the brightness of a lightbulb depend on?

VARIATION IN BRIGHTNESS

You need:
- 4.5-volt battery
- lightbulb with bulb holder
- electric cable
- piece of lead for a mechanical pencil
- tape

What to do:

1 Connect the wire to the battery and to the lightbulb, as on page 27.

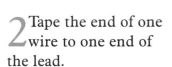

2 Tape the end of one wire to one end of the lead.

3 Run the loose end of wire along the length of the lead.

What happens?
When the end of the wire is run along the length of the lead, the brightness of the light changes.

Why?
As we have already seen, graphite offers resistance to the passage of electrical current. The longer the length of the lead that is part of the circuit, the more energy that is absorbed, and the dimmer the bulb becomes.

Fuses
Electrical items are equipped with small safety devices called fuses. Inside a fuse there is a thin filament that breaks when a current that is stronger than the circuit can support tries to flow through. As the filament breaks, the fuse opens the circuit and interrupts the flow of current. Fuses are like automatic switches that stop the flow of electricity. Without them, the excessive heat in the circuit could cause a fire.

Volts and amps
The electrical force—the force with which the electrical charge passes through a conductor—is measured in volts. On the batteries used in experiments and those that power electrical items and toys, the number of volts is always indicated (1.5V, 4.5V, or 9V). Batteries are not dangerous because of their low voltage. But the current flowing through the wires of electrical installations in the home, which is 110 or 220 volts, can kill a person. The high-tension wires that transport electricity across long distances have a voltage that can exceed 250,000 volts. The speed with which an electric current flows through a wire is measured in amperes (amps for short). An ammeter indicates how many electrical charges pass through a conductor in a certain period of time.

LIKE A FUSE

You need:
- three 4.5-volt batteries
- low-wattage lightbulb with bulb holder
- electric cable, with ends uncovered as before
- small piece of wood
- two metal thumbtacks
- strip of aluminum foil
- pencil sharpened at both ends
- tape

What to do:

1 Connect the batteries together with the wiring. Make sure that the poles that are connected have opposite signs.

2 Push the thumbtacks into the wood. Connect them to the outer battery contacts and to the lightbulb.

3 With two more lengths of wiring, connect the two thumbtacks to the points of the pencil.

What happens?
The bulb gives out a rather dim light.

Why?
The lead of the pencil resists the passage of the current.

4 Put the strip of foil across the two thumbtacks.

What happens?
The bulb produces a bright light and then goes out.

Why?
The strip of foil directly connects the bulb to the batteries, as a parallel circuit. Therefore the bulb lights up with considerable brightness. However, the three batteries (each 4.5 volts) provide the low-wattage bulb with a current that is too strong. Therefore the bulb's filament breaks, interrupting the circuit.

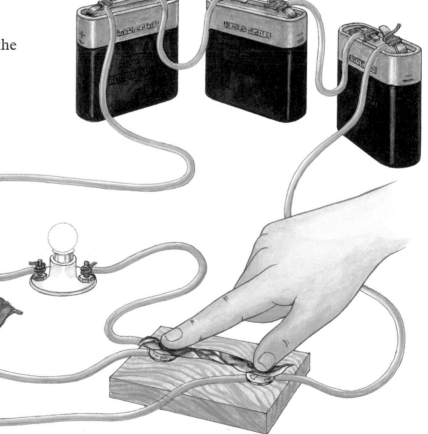

The brightness of a light depends on the speed with which the electrical current flows through the conducting wires.

What does electricity do to water?

CHEMICAL REACTIONS

You need:
- electric cable (with ends stripped)
- two 4.5-volt batteries
- two large screws
- a glass
- water
- salt
- old postcard

What to do:

1 Connect the batteries with a piece of wire. (Connect a negative pole to a positive pole.)

2 Connect each of the outer battery contacts to a screw, as shown.

3 Fill the glass with water. Add some salt.

4 Make two holes in the card, a short distance apart. Place the card on the glass. Thread the screws through the holes.

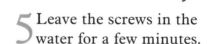

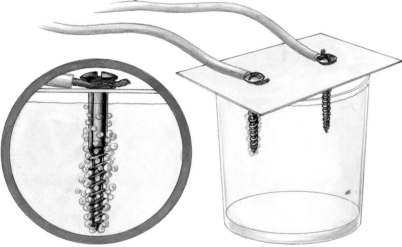

What happens?
Bubbles form around one of the screws.

5 Leave the screws in the water for a few minutes.

What happens?
On the bottom of the glass a green substance is deposited.

6 Take the screws out of the water.

What happens?
The green substance remains on the bottom of the glass.

Why?
Chemical changes are caused by the passage of electrical current through water. The current breaks up the water. (The bubbles are full of hydrogen, a component of water.) The electricity also changes the salt and the iron from the screws into other substances. This is the reason for the discoloration of the water and the deposit on the bottom of the glass.

Electrolysis

The term *electrolysis* means "breaking down through electricity." This is what we call the phenomenon by which the elements of a chemical compound can be separated by the passage of current.

In industry, electrolysis is used to coat metal objects with a layer of another ornamental or protective metal, like gold, silver, or chrome. The object being covered, such as a teaspoon to be plated with silver, is suspended by an electrode (one of the terminals of an electrical circuit) and immersed in a liquid solution that contains silver. Another electrode is also immersed in the liquid. With the passage of the current, the particles of silver become separated into the solution and become attached to the teaspoon. Electrolysis is also used to extract aluminum from rocks and to purify metals, separating the metal particles from the impurities. In car batteries, electrolysis enables electrical energy to be transformed into chemical energy that is stored in the battery. Often the steel bodywork of cars is plated by electrolysis with a thin layer of metal such as zinc to protect it from rust.

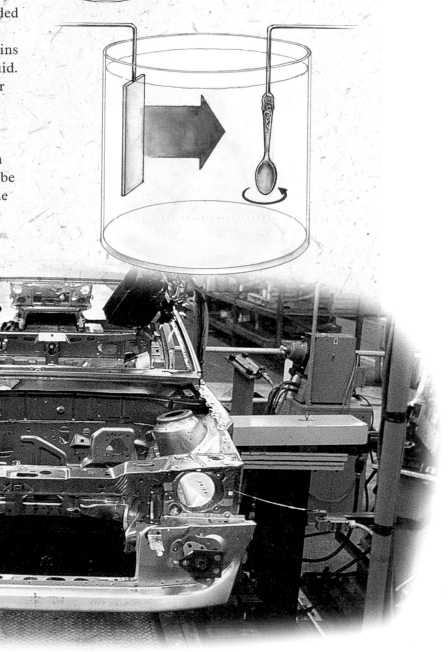

The steel bodywork of cars is often coated with a thin layer of metal such as zinc as protection against rust.

When electricity passes through water it can break up and change the substances that the water contains.

How a battery works

The ordinary dry cell battery works on the same principle as the battery invented by Volta. The battery contains a chemical called manganese dioxide and a chemical paste called the electrolyte. The casing of the battery is made of zinc, and this constitutes the negative pole. At the center of the battery there is a stick of carbon that works as the positive pole. It is connected to the metal cap at the top of the battery. When the battery is connected to a circuit, the chemical substances inside react with one another. This chemical reaction causes the separation of the negative charges from the positive charges, and a flow of current builds up. When the manganese dioxide inside the battery is used up, the battery is "dead" and unusable, unless it is a rechargeable battery.

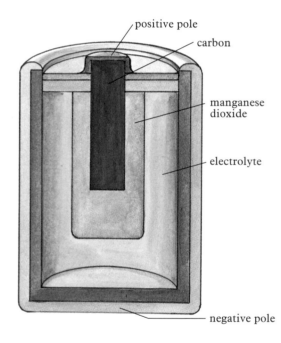

positive pole
carbon
manganese dioxide
electrolyte
negative pole

An electric shock in the sea

The stingray is a fish with a special defense—an electric shock. On the sides of its body, the stingray has two organs made of a special muscle fiber that can accumulate electricity and give off a considerable electric shock, enough to kill or to stun a fish. The stingray is not the only "electric" fish. The manta ray, the electric eel, and other species have organs that can give electric shocks. A shock from an electric eel is strong enough to kill a person.

Inside the plug

An electrical plug is covered with insulating rubber. But the metal prongs allow the current to flow along the wire and power whatever is connected to the electrical supply.

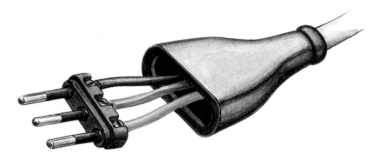

Why we need to strip the ends of wiring

In some of the experiments, you were told to ask an adult to uncover the ends of the electric cable so that you could connect it to a battery or a lightbulb. Electric cable is always covered with insulating plastic. The thin copper filaments inside conduct the current. If the plastic at the ends of the wire is not stripped off, the copper cannot make contact with the battery contacts, nor with the metal parts of the lightbulb. The current would not be able to pass through, because it would be blocked by the plastic. Some other advice:

If you twist the uncovered ends of the copper wire to obtain a stiff and tight end, the wire will be easier to work with. If you need to connect a wire to a battery for only a short time, twist the copper filaments together, then wind them into a small ring that you can thread onto the battery contact and lift back off.

Metric Conversion Table

When you know:	Multiply by:	To find:
inches (in.)	2.54	centimeters (cm)
feet (ft.)	0.3048	meters (m)
yards (yd.)	0.9144	meters (m)
miles (mi.)	1.609	kilometers (km)
square feet (sq. ft.)	0.093	square meters (m^2)
square miles (sq. mi.)	2.59	square kilometers (km^2)
acres	0.405	hectares (ha)
quarts (qt.)	0.946	liters (l)
gallons (gal.)	3.785	liters (l)
ounces (oz.)	28.35	grams (g)
pounds (lb.)	0.454	kilograms (kg)
tons	0.907	metric tons (t)

To convert degrees Fahrenheit (°F) to degrees Celsius (°C), subtract 32, then multiply by $\frac{5}{9}$.

Glossary

ampere (amp): the unit used to measure the strength of an electrical current

atom: the smallest part of a chemical element that has all the properties of that element

attraction: a force that pulls two objects towards each other

charge: an amount of electricity

circuit: the path of an electrical current

conductor: a substance that allows electricity to travel through it

current: the flow of electricity through a wire or other conductor

electron: a tiny particle that moves around the nucleus of an atom. Electrons have a negative electrical charge.

electroscope: device used for detecting a positive or negative electrical charge

fuse: a safety device used in electrical equipment that cuts off the power if something goes wrong

induction: the creation of an electrical charge in an object by bringing the object near an existing electric charge

insulator: a substance that does not let electricity pass through

lightning: a flash of light in the sky caused by electricity moving between clouds or between a cloud and the ground

lightning rod: a metal pole used to attract and carry away the electrical charge from lightning so that it does not damage a building

parallel circuit: a type of circuit in which each part can receive power even when other parts are not being used

potential difference: the difference in charge between one object and another

repel: to push away

resistance: the power of a substance to oppose the flow of electrical current and in that way create heat

series circuit: a type of circuit in which all of the electricity passes through each part of the circuit, one after the other

static electricity: electric charges that build up in an object. Static electricity can be produced when one object rubs against another.

switch: device that opens, closes, or changes the path of an electric circuit

volt: unit for measuring the force of an electrical current or the stored power of a battery

For Further Reading

Asimov, Isaac. *Asimov's Chronology of Science and Discovery*. New York: HarperCollins, 1994.

DiSpezio, Michael Anthony. *Awesome Experiments in Electricity & Magnetism*. New York: Sterling Publications, 2000.

Fleisher, Paul. *Waves: Principles of Light, Electricity, and Magnetism*. Minneapolis: Lerner Publications Company, 2002.

Good, Keith. *Zap It!: Exciting Electricity Activities*. Minneapolis: Lerner Publications Company, 1999.

Himrich, Brenda L., and Stew Thornley. *Electrifying Medicine*. Minneapolis: Lerner Publications Company, 1995.

Kramer, Stephen. *Lightning*. Minneapolis. Carolrhoda Books, Inc., 1992.

Parker, Steve. *Eyewitness: Electricity*. London: DK Publishing, 2000.

Wood, Robert W. *Who?: Famous Experiments for the Young Scientist*. Philadelphia: Chelsea House Publishers, 1999.

Websites

Cool Science, sponsored by the U.S. Department of Energy
<http://www.fetc.doe.gov/coolscience/index.html>

The Franklin Institute Science Museum online
<http://www.fi.edu/tfi/welcome.html>

NPR's *Sounds Like Science* site
<http://www.npr.org/programs/science>

PBS's *A Science Odyssey* site
<http://www.pbs.org/wgbh/aso>

Science Learning Network
<http://www.sln.org>

Science Museum of Minnesota
<http://www.smm.org>

Index

Photo Acknowledgments

The photographs in this book are reproduced by permission of: ©Howard Ande, 4; Romano, L., 5; Archivio IGDA, 6; ©Howard Ande, 14–15; Dagli Orti G., 17; Grazia Neri/M. Agliolo, 18–19; Dani, C., 24; Pozzoni, C., 25; Cigolini, G., 28; Hanson, R., 31; Dagli Orti A., 33a; Vergani, A., 33b. Corbis Royalty Free Images, front cover (top); Todd Strand/Independent Pictures Service, front cover (bottom), back cover (bottom).

Illustrations by Pier Giorgio Citterio.

About the Author

Antonella Meiani is an elementary schoolteacher in Milan, Italy. She has written several books and has worked as a consultant for many publishing houses. With this series, she hopes to offer readers the opportunity to have fun with science, to satisfy their curiosity, and to learn essential concepts through the simple joy of experimentation.